On Poetry and Writing

Encouragement, inspiration and examples for aspiring writers and poets

Eduard Schmidt-Zorner

ISBN: 978-81-19654-05-5

Cover by Jens Rusch (German Artist) from Brunsbüttel (Title: Pisa Study)

First Edition: 2024
Rs. 200/-

Cyberwit.net
HIG 45 Kaushambi Kunj, Kalindipuram
Allahabad - 211011 (U.P.) India
http://www.cyberwit.net
Tel: +(91) 9415091004
E-mail: info@cyberwit.net

Printed at Repro India Limited.

To my wife Marian, a Kerrywoman,
who supports me with patience

FOREWORD

My objective has always been to encourage, motivate, and inspire others to write poems and short stories.

Just as everyone can speak, so everyone can write.

Thus, everyone is a writer and a poet.

Even without being aware of it, we often tell our own stories, share experiences, joys, and sorrows, which can be therapeutic. Writing is therapeutic.

I enjoy writing haibun.

Haibun is a Japanese form of concise short story with a haiku at the beginning, middle, or end. It is a three-line poem that follows a tight tradition. Thus, it imposes a certain "control" that is helpful if you are a "chaotic" person, like me!

I have been published worldwide in over two hundred literary journals and anthologies, and if I can do it, believe me, so can you!

People interested in poetry have often asked me, "How do you write poetry?"

My answer is: "Look inside yourself. What are you carrying in there that you want to let out? What do you want to get rid of? A burden that surfaced recently, an experience that remained in your memory, or a travel encounter? An encounter with a person?

When you have an idea, an inspiration for what to write, sit down and write it as a letter to a stranger—the reader.

Of course, a prerequisite to writing is to read. Not copy, but practice playing the piano keys of language, and be prepared to create the music with your own words and notes. Learn to transform your feelings and thoughts into written words.

You will develop your own style.

Neither fear nor underestimate yourself.

I started with short stories and occasional poems. English is not my native language; writing in another language has challenges. But I got great support from fellow writers and poets.

On my travels, I connected with other poets and writers, attended readings, lectures, and workshops, and presented my literary works to an audience.

Over time, you will grow into this profession.

You will write, discard, rewrite, revise, let your writing rest, pick it up again, and view it anew.

The task is a joy because it is creative, and creativity should never lie idle.

This publication shares my experience and feelings and will give you inspiration, ideas, and example how to write without being academic and without being didactic.

Start to write.

Here are ten writing tips:

1. Read as much as possible. Analyse your liking for a certain style.
2. Do your research. Study all forms of prose and poetry.
3. Find someone who inspires you — A writer, dead or alive.
4. Attend readings, join writer groups, read, read, read.
5. Writers write. Period. Start to write. Prose or poetry.
6. Do not be downhearted when it does not work at the beginning.
7. Be authentic and deliberate — do not copy or imitate. Do not use AI.
8. Tell stories that hook people. Talk to people and find out what people are interested in.
9. Read your works repeatedly and improve, delete, add.
10. A word on grammar - use it well.

Contents

Berlin

We, a Russian friend, and me, sat in a café in *Charlottenburg* on a very grey, muggy August afternoon in 1999. The quarter was also called *Charlottengrad*, as in the twenties, because of the many Russian emigrants at that time and now again.
"Your poems show trepidation… fear," I remarked.
He raised his head, and there was nothing but emptiness in his grey Russian eyes as he said:
"Do you think my new poems reflect that? It's all said, isn't it? Why is man afraid, and where does this fear originate?"
His poems, as good as Russian poems had been for a long time, are realistic, profound, and exciting to the point of breakdown, and they speak about his people and his family.
"Do you want another coffee?" I asked.
I looked past him onto the street, and suddenly, I imagined everything in black and white as in an old photo: the passers-by, the shop windows, the trees. The men wore black hats, the women long, heavy dresses, old *Horch* limousines and trams drove by, and every second passer-by spoke a beautiful, old-fashioned, pre-revolutionary Russian.
"Yes, tea would be fine," he said, bringing me back to reality from a sudden dream. As a coffee addict, I forgot that Russians are tea drinkers.
"When one writes," I said, "one should strive to make the world better with words because we are lucky enough to live in a world that is much better than it was a hundred years ago. And this despite the many international conflicts.
"Russia has not changed for centuries, and the best people have died. Or they left the country forever. Is this a poetry of defeat?" he asked.

Afterwards - by now, the world was back in colour - we talked about literature. *Nabokov*, *Varlam Shalamov's* Gulag stories; also raved about *Proust* and *Updike*.

He mentioned a photo of his family that he had recently found in an album, a photo from 1914.

"None of them died like human beings; they perished during the Civil War, under Stalin, in besieged *Leningrad*, in the Gulags."

He paused for a long time, and I noticed how pale, tired, and sad he was—a man in his mid-50s who had aged too soon.

"I only want to live longer than these people in the photo and those in my poems."

And then suddenly, the sky opened and sunbathed the white tablecloths on the café tables in a warm, optimistic light.

Sowing Expressiveness

People spread many things:
Viruses, bacteria, rumours, bad smells.
But poetry has a positive contagion.
I want to spread this addiction,
find like-minded rhymers,
just like pot-heads
who roam the coffee shops,
near *Amsterdam's* canals.

I want to raise this subject,
provoke a discussion
on this enchanting addiction,
in a disenchanted world
to heel wounded souls,
foster creativity, exchange words
with related minds,
to chisel verses and stanzas.

A suitable place is a café,
always has been, or a patisserie.
World literature, many novels,
were written on café tables,
in side-lanes in *Paris*,
in *Dublin* and *New York City*
where authors get imagination
and manifold inspiration.

Visiting my old hometown,
I head for my favourite café.

A new face behind the counter.
She was Turkish, a new encounter.
She wanted to write too, she said.
Go ahead, I responded.
I told her about my time in *Istanbul*
and the art of haiku.

I wrote an example in her language,
told her that my prose and poetry
was imbued with this "*Hüzün*",
collective feeling, romantic melancholy,
a literary tristesse
found in songs and poems
of a sleepwalkers' town
İstanbul'da bir güz. *

She knew what I was talking about
and understood my love for Istanbul,
listened to my poems and *haibun*
about the old Bosporus quarters,
the alleys, the Byzantine walls,
the *Tarlabaşı* Boulevard, a *medress*
next to a caravansary,
lined with old mulberry trees.

I try to kindle this desire
to make people write
to express their innermost
emerging before our eyes
like a plant that grows.
All should seek and find.
That's why I exude enthusiasm,
and joy about the written rhythm.

Absence of a Poet

His absence unnoticed,
he liked to write poems
on white birch bark,
catch the intuition spark
between midnight
and four in the morning
or
between lilac and elderflower
when the sun is shining.

He was noticed when *Charon*,
the ferryman of *Hades*,
rows him to the other side,
across the rivers *Styx and Acheron*
as so many before him.

He could not pay his *obol*
and wanders the shores for
one hundred years, leaving
poem sheets as marks
on the everchanging sand.

Weight of a Poem

This poem is light,
it weighs one gram,
the weight of the paper,
it's written on.

Piece of paper, handmade,
then cut with a blade,
moving in the gentle breeze,
taking off, tumbling over the trees,
it is so light, light as a feather…
carried away
out of sight, but not out of mind.

A poem chiselled in stone is indelible.
Such poems are durable.
Its title on the epitaph
is etched into a copper sheet,
prone to *verdigris*,
creating green letters,
pretending eternal youth.

A poem on sand is transient,
it vanishes….
Words blown away by the wind
or flowing with the waves,
extinguished by the turn of the tide,
entangled in the reeds of our brain
they hide.

Thoughts put into a poem
some are light, some are heavy,
but still, the words move with our breath
into infinity, where stars
that died millions of years ago,
cast their light, light, lightly
on poets like us,
light as the poem in our hand,
which weighs a gram
and has no end.

Deficiency of a Foreign Poet

Helpless in the workshop, I stand.
All have a potter's wheel and tools at hand.
There's a trough with clay.
All work away.

They shape and form with a light touch.
I have no potter's wheel or turning table as such.
The others have a modelling stick, wire loop, a tool.
I have but an old, rough wooden spoon.

Wooden like my tongue, imperfect, bumpy,
the turnout is strange and clumsy.
I am not able to form and shape a text,
cannot bring word fragments into context.

The others have round pots of a beautiful form.
Mine is crooked, looking forlorn.

Now I try the tailor's shop to stitch a text,
and look perplexed.
There's a dress form with a pinned skirt, the latest fashion.
All have scissors, patterns, and pincushion.

I have but a measuring tape,
to measure - that it is not enough.
Skill, elegance, and intuition are missing.

It remains a crooked pot,
an unfinished frock.

Continuation

The best poems have long been written.
Why am I sitting under my bookshelf,
trying to reinvent the wheel,
staring at my pen?
Only because a book fell on my head?
Yeats…on the spine,
in golden letters.

The best paintings have been painted.
Hanging in museums with all that has been created.
Why am I sitting in front of my easel and
dip the brush into the paint?
Only because I knocked my head on the frame
when I wanted to read the information plate.
Chagall, his birth date,
in small print.

The best songs have been composed and played.
Why should I sing loud in an empty place,
unwanted melodies sung by an untrained voice,
given such a choice of famous songs?
Only because a melody sounds
in my confused head?

Why being downhearted,
why not
following in the footsteps
of poets and painters?
Why not search in our heart's depth,

what motivated those writers?
They are dead; we are still alive.

So why should we not strive
to continue their way,
by night and by day?
Why not join the endless queue
of versifiers and bards,
of painters and artists
singers and daubers?

Others will follow us.
Let's be adventurous!
Inventive. Creative. Immortal.
Something remains.

Words in abeyance

When I arrived in Paris in 2019, I had only looked for a short-term accommodation, which I found in the 9th arrondissement, but ended up staying longer than expected in that quarter.

The morbid romantic atmosphere, rising streets, lanterns, a railway bridge that announced the nearby *Gare du Nord*, flaking house fronts, dark corners, and old trees all captivated me.

The 9th arrondissement was one of those quarters where I felt at home from the moment of my arrival. Bistros, cafés, pubs side by side. They are not luxurious or trendy, but a place for residents who visit them out of boredom or loneliness, to take their lunch breaks or have a rest after work. One queues up in the same bakery shop, buys in the same tobacco shop, browses the newspapers in the newspaper stand, and waves bonjour when entering the bistro.
I did not attract particular attention in the bistro when I came home from work in the evening with traces of flour on my hands and hair because I had to learn how to bake baguettes and croissants in *Grands Moulins de Paris* as a prerequisite of my new job.

Most memorable were the faces of the people I saw every evening. I sat there often and wrote. There was enough inspiration. I caught snippets of conversations, and this kindled my fantasy. I wrote and wrote, scribbled short stories and poems. I read in their faces, which were full of untold stories, and I tried to give them a voice. I wrote occasionally for the Renault News.

Some guests asked me what I was writing. I said, "I write about you." They said, "How can you write about us? You do not know us." They asked to hear my stories. And they exclaimed, "But that is my life."

Months later, I moved into an apartment in the 6th arrondissement, a different neighbourhood on the other side of the Seine.
I went through all the trendy bistros and cafés in the quarter near *St Germain de Prés*. While searching for a new "favourite" bistro, I opened the doors, pretending to look for someone. In seconds, I knew if I suited the place, and the place suited me.

I found such a bistro. Old world style, cosy, comfortable corners, quiet, not overcrowded.
A few guests had a book or a magazine in front of them; others looked out the window at the passers-by. What struck me was that I didn't see faces. I saw faces, but they were not the ones in the 9th arrondissement that would grasp my attention. Faces with an open expression that told a story, a desire, a fate. Here, the faces were shields that said: Do not disturb.

I paid more attention to the hands that spoke volumes. They were not the hands of workers, shopkeepers, cleaners, or brick-layers; they were fine hands, the hands of the bourgeoisie.

They were well-groomed and well-manicured, some with rings, some without.

At the table next to me sat a lady holding a small music book. I glimpsed the title. *Chopin – Étude Op. 10 No. 4.*
I remembered that this piece, marked *presto con fuoco*, demands a fast pace and requires constant fluidity in both hands.

She had those tender piano hands that fly over the ivories like a weaver's shuttle.

I sent a smile over to her. No reaction.
I noticed this phenomenon very often. Hesitant, sparing handling of feelings, controlled.

A poem had built up in my brain, and I put it on paper.

Saving bank of feelings

We meet people
who divide their emotions
in small portions
rationalize their smiles,
their empathy and feelings,
not to release too much energy.

They see their body
as a non-rechargeable battery.
They drown
in their unspent feelings.

I paid and left the sheet of paper behind me.

When I passed the window, I saw the lady taking the paper from the table and reading the poem.

Last Lines

The piazza groaned under the evening glow.

Was it wasting the last minutes of life
or gaining some time
when he was asked what his last wish
was and
he answered: “To write a poem”?

The officer behind the table nodded in
consent and the priest in his black soutane
coughed apprehensively into his handkerchief.

The characters on the paper were black
when the death squad officer raised
his gloved hand and barked:

“Ready” and ”Fire”.

The poem had a preliminary end.
A lonely line hung over the heart-breaking scene.
And the characters changed to blood-red
on the wall.

Pegasus*

A rider's silhouette
emerging from the night
pulled into dawn,
he walks, lost his white horse,
against the snowy backdrop of vast plains,
drags himself to the forest's edge.
A white sheet of paper tumbles down,
he takes the feather of a crow
and with his heart blood, he writes down,
forlorn, the pain of losing his stallion.
Its name was "*Pegasus*."
A writer now was born.
A story
to transform reality
to bear a dream of literacy.

Peaceful Land Seizure

I'd like to write poetry,
which opens the door,
slightly.

Push it open yourself.
Go out, peaceful be your land seizure.
Pour yourselves the purest wine
and leave no doubts,
and rehearse the upright walk.

Find the point, always the one,
where you gently unhinge the world.

Penwordflow

The night
shared an hour of writing with me.
"Write," said the night....
And I said, obediently, "Right".
Between 4 and 5 a.m. is my creative time.
The brain's resting time
creates a rhyme.
Awoke from a dream or slumber,
groped for the light switch
in the dark,
hark, a brilliant idea came up,
and a pen in standby mode,
conserves the thought,
a poem, haibun or an ode
on a piece of paper.

Advert

I forgot to tell you,
that I found abducted words,
at the roadside.
You left a message,
but I erased the tape:
there was nothing on it
but headache
and love talked to pieces.

Look, it's still there,
remained untouched,
because it's hard to handle:
Empathy and sensitivity.

Now, I am looking for
something with a quality seal
and without a bitter aftertaste
of secondary thoughts.

I search for someone,
during rainy days,
who asks me about poetry,
takes poems apart with me
and analyses them over a coffee.

Maybe you will get back to me?

Love is proven with a poem.

Since Éric moved to Paris, he still could not get used to the buzzing, underlying background noise and the soundscape of a big city that swells and intensifies around midnight. Being alone enhanced his perception of sounds and made him listen into the night. Before he stepped out onto the street in the morning, he knocked at the concierge's window. She handed him his mail without saying a word.

A week ago, she told him a lady had left greetings and a message. Of course, the concierge had the intention to convey the greetings, but when the woman had left the house, she had forgotten - the woman and her name - not the message, which was: 'Nobody picks up the phone. Can you tell him to answer the phone?'

The concierge tried to remember: The name had been something like Béatrice. The woman quickly had turned away and left in a rush.

Éric did not know any Béatrice.

So far, he has not received a call on his mobile. It must have been an old acquaintance who still had his landline number. He went through similar-sounding names: Denice? Héloïse? Catrice?

Éric went into the confectionery shop across the street, owned by an Algerian. The television in the back room, which one could see when standing at the table by the window, showed a *Raï music* program on *Canal Algérie*. He loved the sound and rhythm.

He ordered a coffee and flatbread with quince, - fig-, and morello cherries jam and read his mail.

There was a picture postcard of the *Brandenburg Gate*. A card from Darcie.

'I hope this message reaches you. Are you still living at the same address? Maybe I will be back in Paris in spring.'

There was also a letter from his cousin. He had married a young Moroccan woman in Casablanca. The man was in his seventies. My God, is there no end? It was his fourth marriage after having been divorced three times. The usual male battle against age, physical decay, and death.

He opened a violet envelope sent by Eléonore, written in her purple ink. The letter was short, like a haiku:

you limp behind time
walk blindly through your life and mine
fallen out of time

Éric smiled. She was a literary talent but a bit overpowering and patronizing.

On his days off from work, he liked to walk from his apartment down to the Seine.
A habit he repeated three uneventful days and restless nights later.

Éric bought cigarettes and matches at a kiosk, opened the packet, and lit a *Gauloise*.

He loved those days without any commitments, sitting on the banks of the *Seine*, watching the boats passing and looking across to the other side of the river, at the houses, the linden trees, and the artists with their easels.

Éric also loved the quiet evenings, where he would sit in front of a café at a round marble table on a cobblestone side street and rest in the cool-soothing scent of mimosa trees and honeysuckle. He loved to walk from café to café like the 'Stations of the Cross', drinking a café or pastis here and there, and moving on to the next café where he read a newspaper that somebody had left.

He glanced at the crossword puzzles, a serial, and the horoscope columns.
He skimmed the section with his sign:
'You will have a re-encounter that will open a new door in your life.'
He smirked. 'What a load of nonsense.'

He leaned back and enjoyed the scenery. Football fans wearing pointed caps and scarves from *Paris Saint-Germain* and *AS Saint-Etienne* football clubs sang their songs on their way to a game.

Eric had planned to eat at his favourite restaurant, *Jardin Notre-Dame*, near *Quai de Montebello*. As he left the *Quai Saint-Michel* metro station, he saw Héloïse on the other side of the street. In a flash, he recalled their relationship as uncomplicated and positive. Éric was attracted to intellectual women. Héloïse was an independent woman and did not impose her lifestyle on others. She loved his poetry, which flattered him. He liked her and was pleased to see her again after over six months.

He waved and called her name. She did not see him—or did she not want to see him?
He ran across the street without watching the traffic. A car had to make an emergency stop. The driver shouted, "Idiot," and tapped his forehead. Passers-by shook their heads.

He called again, "Héloïse." She stopped and turned, "Ah, Éric. *Quelle surprise*."

"Did you inquire about me a week ago? My concierge told me about a lady's visit."

"No, probably another one of your ex-lovers. There are obviously some with whom I share the same fate. I don't seem to be the only one in your life."

"You were my only one, but you let our relationship grow cold. I have never forgotten you."

"**I** let it grow cold? **You** have let it peter out. It was not my fault; I think you are commitment phobic."

"I am on the way to the Restaurant *Jardin*. May I invite you?"

"No, I have to attend a conference in the *Sorbonne*; I only have half an hour."

"OK, then let's go to *La Crème de Paris*. They have a lovely selection of crêpes and cakes. Their *café liégeois* is heavenly."

She sat opposite him and looked at him. Her face was like a marble statue of a Madonna, framed by black hair and with green, radiant eyes.

“You’ve got a few grey hairs”, she remarked.

“You have not changed. I have missed you. I still often dream of our time together.”

“Oh, you are so romantic.”

“What about a new beginning?”

“New? What does that mean? Isn’t a beginning always new? You mean continuation, to start where we stopped. I warn you; I have commitments. By the way, I got the professorship at the Faculty of Humanities.”

There was her seductive, magic look: “But I will not make it easy for you. You must suffer a bit.
Let us do it like in fairy tales when the admirer of a princess performs tasks or has to go through dangerous adventures to win the princess’s hand. I will not go so far, but… write me a poem that shows how much you love and desire me, and we will see. Email it to me; I still have the same address.”

She looked at her watch.

“I have to go. I am waiting for your poem.”
She breathed a kiss on his cheek.

“Wait,” Éric said, “I go with you; I enjoy every minute with you.”

Eric accompanied her down *Rue du Petit Pont,* and they parted in front of Restaurant *Jardin* with its yellow-green marquise. The scent of her perfume rested in the air for a while.

The tasty food and the double espresso with a glass
of *Calvados* stimulated Éric's brain.
He wrote his thoughts on the notepad of his mobile phone:

Restart

A soothing night
covers a humming metropolis,
it blankets the quarters,
its banlieues.
Lone men and women,
alone among millions,
lost in a sea of lights,
and night-shaded alleys.

I found my counterpart,
and hold her hand.
Lips meet.
The scent of vanilla and herbs.
I discover oases and hills,
valleys with all their secrets.

I play with her on mystic strings,
unlock unknown sounds
which dissolve,
fade like the melodic clink
of piano tunes
evoked by black-white ivories.

Your breath in my ear,
words whispered into your hair,
we sink into love,
and drown
in a warm embrace.
Your lips entice me

to kiss ripe fruits
from cherry branches.

Ittar*,
made from the essence,
of roses, herbs, and spices.
A drop on your lips,
a drop on my skin.
You are like the wine
from the Languedoc
a taste on my tongue,
overwhelming, floral, ripe,
the taste of the autumn sun.

The silvery play of the moon over the silk tides of the Seine had a dreamy effect on Éric.
He took the metro back to the ninth arrondissement.

Back in his apartment he opened his laptop, transferred the poem from the notepad, went through it a few times, and sent it to Héloïse.

"Voilà," he said contentedly to himself.

He uncorked a bottle of wine, leafed through *Michel Houellebecq's* anthology of poems, and concluded that he wrote better poetry.

When he was preparing for bed, he heard the sound of an incoming message on his laptop.

Héloïse had responded:

“Cherie, your poem warmed my heart. What do you think about me cooking something next weekend? *Cassoulet Gratin Dauphinois* that you loved to eat? I have *Auvergne* cheese and a few bottles of *Languedoc-Roussillon* wines left.

And what would you like for breakfast? *Croissants* or *brioche*? Or *pain au chocolat*?

Poetry Metabolism

My idea flows from the brain
through the arm into the pen
on untouched, immaculate paper
to absorb my thoughts
which are beginning to take shape.
Am I satisfied with that sentence,
which was ejaculated on the page?
I see myself in the glass door of the bookcase
and find the picture disgustingly pretentious
a sad appearance.

Now there it lies,
the leaf poem
like a salad dish,
where every leaf gets a meaning
before it is swallowed and digested.
Unpalatable to some people,
will lie heavy in their stomach
for some time.

Portrait of a Poet

What should a poet look like?
Enraptured, ecstatic, mad,
absent-minded, transfigured,
or like a tyke?

What is he supposed to do?
Quoting long dialogues,
a meaningful sentence,
his favourite expression:
Je m'en fiche, (I do not care)
Not sicklied o'er
with the pale cast of thought. *

Sits in his favourite café,
likes to talk,
drinks red wine, hugs a lot,
tells anecdotes from his life,
recites radical verses
that carry death in them,
does not need a scapegoat,
not bothering his neighbourhood.

Holds a notebook tight to his chest,
his memory, his quaint data bank,
a beau laid, handsome for some,
ugly for others,
faithful to his past girlfriends,
the old flames, who ring him,
looking for consolation.

We see him now, old as well,
with an anarchist's beard,
white mane, like a horse,
he creates word formations,
with obsession, is caffeine-addicted,
wears a crinkled grin,
chronically ill of poetry and lyrics.

Kissing hands, old school.
Freethinker, maladjusted,
to fulfil expectations, he failed.
Using the plumb line on himself,
fathoming constantly
and being self-critical.
Poems frequently submitting,
a hundred times rejected.

Delighted to be published,
sets scent marks like a dog.
Lifts his leg in every poet's corner.
Despair is allowed,
discouragement is forbidden.
I see someone in the mirror.
Is it me or who?
Sorry to have bothered you.

*Shakespeare

In the Greenhouse of Poetry

Light as a feather
and free like a bird,
thoughts ruffle,
line up letter by letter,
forming seed rows,
fragments take shape,
grow in fertile dreams.

Word infatuated,
meandering in vagueness,
yet without squiggles,
commenced, virgin still,
unfinished words,
as rustling leaves.

Ploughing word fields,
epically sprawling, word signs,
bog soil on which I try to stand.
One word short
may fit into verses
that lie in wait,
pupated, ramified drawn,
words are waiting for solid ground.

Put lyrical seedlings in brittle brickwork;
they can sprout and germinate in crevices.
I suck honey from paper flowers.

Metrical foot, rhythmically throbbing,
waiting to be broken.
Finished prodigies
finally replanted in anthologies.

Verses in Greenhouses

Lyrical seedlings have many gardeners,
those who sow finely and in equal distance
others dig straight furrows,
those who, with a swift, sweeping motion
scatter the seeds against the wind,
others are breeders who plan carefully
make the seeds sprout with patience,
some prepare the earth meticulously,
compress, level, scarify,
lay out flower beds and draw lines.

This all asks for rules,
which will soon be neglected and broken.
Syllable counters love the gardener's trade,
multicoloured fruits, as alliterations,
cross-, and end rhymes are created,
laboriously rhyming flower with bower
or roses with meadows
to put us in a lyrical mood.

I lean the rake against the fence
and take a rest.
Some things are rooted in flowerpots
or are disposed of in anthologies
until mildew settles
on the evergreen questions.

Word Power

A poet was sent into banishment
by the order of gaffer *Stalin*,
displaced, deported,
marginalized, uprooted,
deprived of his homeland
his breeding ground.

Long train journey, vast land,
forests as far as the eye can see,
snow deserts, unsurmountable rivers,
taiga and tundra, the heart shivers.
Everything has just been an episode,
a fraction of history.

An endless succession of doors,
gradually closed behind him.
Barbed wire along the rail track,
thousands went before him
in this lonely, hostile landscape
into an endless white.

The train passed by camps,
where many were slain.
The screams of the victims
are still stuck in the treetops.
Trees are like crystal structures,
the hope of return is in vain.

The train covered miles,
through wasteland,
and seedless fields
and through deserted plains
past burnt villages.
Like a black and white film.

His friends tried to trace him,
to find his place of exile:
'He who is sought is not lost'.
But there was no hope, no trace.
With closed eyes, one could see
the cycle of hope and despair.

He only had paper and pen
to write everything down.
The dialogue with himself,
the composition of verse,
the silent recitation of a poem
kept him alive.

The wind captured new words,
distributed by the wind.
The wind became redder with time:
Resistance wind.
He grew up in a storm,
ice flowers, his thoughts.

Discovery

I fear that the beating of my heart
might betray what emerges
from unborn, unwritten verses.

My soul-searching
leads far into the distance.
On Canal St Martin, swans proceed;
doves fly overhead.

I tear a piece of dream from dawn,
and put it where hope grows,
forgotten thoughts slumber,
that contradict the daily news.

I turned into *Rue des Récollets*. On the left is Park *Jardin Villemin*. The water of *Canal St. Martin* at the other end of the street reflected the lanterns along the waterway. I parked and walked up the street, which carried the smells of car fumes, fries, dust, and grass and leaves.
It was a quiet evening. No sound could be heard from the nearby *Gare de l'Est*. In the background, a metropolis melody played, humming and whispering.

A friend had recommended a restaurant in this quarter. "*Petite brasserie très sympa*", one could read in Google maps ranking. The place had a distinguished old-world décor with a wooden bar and big windows. There was no Wi-Fi or TV, but the atmosphere was relaxing and invited to dream.
It was ideal for spending a Sunday evening watching the boats

traveling up and down the canal.
The waiter handed me the menu. He wore a black waistcoat, a white shirt, and a long white apron in the traditional style of a Paris waiter.

I ordered a *café au lait* and opened the weekend edition of *Le Parisien*, in which my Lebanese food report was published.

A steaming coffee was served, and I looked out the window. The day had ended, and the sun had set. A boat passed by; the lights of the boats were shining on the water and creating golden circles.

I had just sipped my coffee when a bent man entered the restaurant. I could not judge his age. He passed by the tables and offered a kind of booklet or brochure that looked like a few A5 pages stapled together in the middle.

His worn clothes were a mixture of styles. A blue hooded anorak showed a lot of stains, the lower part of his brown trousers hung in rags around his ankles, and his bare feet were in sandals. He held a knapsack in his hand.

He passed by my table and looked at me. I smiled and said: *Bonsoir*. He seemed surprised and returned my greeting. He cast a desiring glance at my coffee. When the waiter tried to show him the door, I invited him to sit. I told the waiter he was my guest and asked the man what he wanted.

“A coffee and a *brioche* if possible”, he said.

I asked the waiter to bring a big cup of coffee and a *brioche* with butter.

The ‘clochard’ (we say now politically correct: sans domicile fixe. SDF) said to me:
“Excuse me for a moment; I will just wash my hands before I have my coffee.”

He shuffled to the toilet, watched by the waiter and the guests, who frowned or wrinkled their noses when he passed by.

The owner took the opportunity and approached me:
“Please, what you do is not acceptable. We have to show consideration for our guests.”

I felt my blood pressure rising and, emphasizing my point by pounding my finger on the table, I replied:

“I can leave an assessment in ‘*Tripadvisor*’ or put a story into *Le Parisien*, where you can read my weekly restaurant reviews. So, for your record, whatever I order or whatever he orders, you will serve. “

The man returned. His face looked fresher, and he had combed his hair.
After a moment of silence, he drank his coffee and ate his *brioche*.

I told him that he reminded me of *Jean Gabin*, the French actor who played a homeless in *Archimède le Clochard,* a romantic movie far removed from the harsh reality.

He nodded sadly:
“I know the film. There is no romanticism attached to it. To have no money, to live in a homeless shelter, if you are lucky to get a space, especially in winter, to sleep under the bridges, to live in

cardboard boxes, or on top of the outlet shafts of the metro to avail of the warm air or to look for work in the central wholesale market in the early hours of the day, is far removed from romantic feelings, I can assure you."

"I do not want to offend you, but how did you get into this situation and cope with all the prejudice?"

"No offence. The majority are addicted to alcohol and drugs; they are homeless because of a failed relationship, loss of a job, or disastrous financial circumstances; anyone could end one day in a similar situation.
I worked in a sales department and built a house, but the company closed. I lost my job. There was no money to keep up the living standard or pay the mortgage. I got divorced, and the way downhill started rapidly."

I handed him the menu.
"Order whatever you want; you are my guest. I will have a filet of sole with lemon sauce and raspberry *crème brûlée* as dessert."

"Thanks, you put me to shame. I will take the sole as well. No dessert, please."

"Do you need help?" I asked. I have some clothes in the car that might fit you. I think you have my size."

"Thanks, that would be nice."

He looked down at his trousers.
"No harm to get rid of these rags. By the way, my name is Léandre Beauchemin.

"Another prejudice is that we are useless, lazy, unable to cope with our life. I am writing poems and short stories", he said.

He pulled his small booklet out of his knapsack.

"I offer them for a few Euros. They are handwritten. The owner of a copy shop copied them for me free of charge. I sell four or five per day. I have some change. May I invite you for an espresso?"

"With pleasure", I replied. I accepted his invitation to keep his dignity and took his book:

"We are colleagues; I write prose, poetry and reviews for *Le Parisien.*"

I opened the poetry collection at random and read a poem:

The Poor Poet
A poet without abode
constructs an invisible home for himself,
that gives him spiritual shelter.
On paper, he builds an illusory world.
A promise on a white sheet.

He holds his writing quill,
uses his fingers to count the meter.
Shoes with holes in the soles,
to keep in touch with the soil,
socks not been washed for months,
a mixture of second-hand clothes,
a weird fashion.

The constant ticking in his head
Where to find a roof for the night,
where to get a bite
or work to earn a few coins.

When the winter sets in
and the sun lets ice crystals
melt on the windowpane,
which run down like tears,
a white sheet covers the promises again.

This man needs help, I said to myself, and I was determined to support him.

I had an idea:

"How many poems did you write? You could compile a collection. Do you know other homeless who write? We could publish an anthology; the publication will make you known, you and your problems. And a bit of money would be no harm. How can I reach you?"

He gave me the number of a homeless shelter. I gave him my card.

"I often stay in the Park *Villemin* during the day, but please leave a message, and we can meet again," he said.

I drove him to his shelter before midnight after we left the restaurant. The shelter, *Emmaüs*, *Rue de Lancry*, was in a respectable area near *Boulevard de Magenta,* between shops and Italian takeaways. Léandre waved until I was out of sight.

On my way to my apartment in the 9th arrondissement, my thoughts were kindled by the conversation with this unfortunate man.

On my way to my office the next day, I bumped into Marcel Lejeune, a filmmaker. We arranged to meet for lunch.

"Any news, a new project?" was my first question.

"Yes, we want to raise awareness of the problems and talents of the homeless in Paris. Times have gotten tougher for them; the municipality is merciless."

"Hold on," I said, telling him the story of the encounter with Léandre.
He listened with a serious look. After a moment, he said:

"Just the character I am looking for".

Poet

The poet,
so they say,
and it is expected of him,
should be an admonisher
using fine words,
radiate something edifying,
be aesthetic,
even a comic relief,
presenting rhymes
with a wrinkled forehead.

A poet,
it is said,
and also expected,
should be a guide,
a well-worded signpost
in condensed form,
often in epic length.
to speak of pain and joy,
love and death
with a melancholic look.

A poet,
as the expression goes,
and is demanded of him,
is intended as an incentive
an uncomfortable zeitgeist,
with a rhythmic crack of a whip,

striking, succinct,
rolling out life
like dough
and still bakes a sweet cake.

Festina Lente

(make haste slowly)

Some call it deceleration
I find it enriching and accelerating.
Only in silence good things can flourish
haste has never helped anyone,
keeps the pressure and stress anguish.

I sit in my corner and dream,
and crochet and knit
my poems, which,
in silence,
trickle into my undisturbed brain.

There is a tactile arrangement
between pen, paper, and table,
a sorting of word fragments
to enable to line up the terms
and compose a picture
to make it tangible
for the reader.

The Poetry Volume

The postman brought a book
from near *Bremen*, *Worpsweder* land.
Lovingly, elaborately packed
by an antiquarian hand.
The envelope was quickly
torn open by me,
impatiently.

I found the book wrapped
in a newspaper, "*WÜMME REPORT.*"
from Sunday, 14th June 2020.
With local, idyllic news.
Safe world, untouched, unbruised.

Cheesecake recipe, nice living.
Photos of friendly people.
A bit of a gossip in a pleasant dose.
An anniversary mentioned,
the kitten of the year.

Then, I held the poetry book in my hand.
Thin and simple.
This former colleague,
a poet
wrote many poems.

Curiosity and interest combined
were decisive in the purchase.
I met him in the office, the hallway,

at *Hoesch Estel.* A long time ago.
The book of poems, intact virgin.
Meaningful. From a poet colleague.

I don't know if he is still alive.
I don't think so; he'd be 101.
No trace on the World Wide Web.
Did I wake the dead?
Woke them up? Did I startle them?

Who will turn back, was the title
by *Dr Hans Schaller.*

The translation of one of his stanzas:

Auf dem steilen, steinern' Wege
schritt ein Paar den Wald empor,
Hand in Hand, bis es sich später
in der Einsamkeit verlor…

On a steep and stony path
a couple up the forest walks
hand in hand, until they later
got lost in solitude...

Font and typesetting

We poets and writers owe a lot to the art of printing—actually, everything.
Printing transports us into the outside world where we can share our fantasies and thoughts with the reader.

I spent hours and days in a printing workshop in *Hoya*, in the flat countryside, a town on the river *Weser* in *Lower Saxony*, and contemplate and watched the master of the printing works, the typesetter. He printed posters for an exhibition that day. Followed by a text for a small poetry volume.

The thought of the typesetting with its smell of lead, dust, and paint recalls the movement of the typesetter's hand between the typesetting box and the angle hook, a flying movement of a weaver's shuttle. A busy hand.
And the letters, lined up, side by side, turned into complete words, then lines. Little by little, the sentence came into the galley, which holds the type for a whole page.

I remember the shape of the letters. The most beautiful were those with wings on the strokes, called *serifs*. The writing was called *Antiqua*. The wingless ones were called *Grotesque*. There were many different fonts. Names like *Garamond, Bodoni, and Gill* slip from my memory. I liked *Palatino* best, with the beautiful S, like a swan.

The fonts were divided into points according to size. The most common was the ten-point, called *Corpus*. *Cicero* was the twelve-point. Eight was the *Petit*, which was primarily used in tables. To set books, compose words, print texts—thick books, poems, novels, announcements, posters, and leaflets—is an art.

Today, we use film typesetting. The machines became museum pieces.

Typesetting

She had those tender piano hands,
hands which fly over the ivories
like a weaver's shuttle.
Hit the keys, the black and white,
like a typesetter moves
between box
and the angle hook
to compose a line.
Wandering hands.

And the notes look like *serifs*
with wings on the strokes
and the *Palatino*,
with the beautiful S,
like a swan's neck,
notes, which are a sound
and tone.

The *Cosmos* flowers in the garden:
violet, white, pink
add to the ivory and black.
Smell and music merge
like paper and ink,
and a song emerges
and a poem is created.

On a New Page.

I had a specific idea
before my mind's eye.
An idea, maybe a crazy one,
born from a dream in a restless night.

I woke up and put it on paper.
Words were whispered,
light as a feather, free as a bird,
words which go astray
or fall into oblivion
if not written down instantly.

Some of them ruffle their feathers
and are soon forgotten
others lead to serious type cases,
letter after letter, typesetting.

Word-infatuated as I am,
meandering between lines,
densely written rows of notes,
illegible in the morning.

What began remains unfinished.
Worn words, worn down, worn out,
or remain silent, leave no trace.
Evergreen word tirades pass quickly,
they wither or manifest themselves,
become a cuckoo's egg in the composition,
unfit for epic proliferation.

'Age-shrewd' I turn the hourglass.
Forging is too loud for a wordsmith.
I weave with a light hand as
weaver of words,
to lie to the time, to interlace the minutes,
to form poems that cast no shadows.

A Poem for Africa

Edmond's mobile rang. It was Mamadou Assamoua, his girl-friend, his poet soul mate, and head of the Club *Littéraire* in Paris.

"You won't believe it. I got an invitation from our Embassy for a literature event in two weeks' time."

"Great", Edmond said, "congratulations."

"I was told to bring a male friend or my partner along. Maybe a single woman means danger at those events."

"Would not surprise me," Edmond sneered.

"And the guests are asked to contribute with a piece of prose, poetry or music."

"They could not have chosen a more capable person than you."

Mamadou said, "I will definitely not contribute anything. But you should present your poem on Africa."

"I will think about it. It may be too provocative."

"Poems have to be provocative", she said. "Air your black suit."

"It's always aired; you know that I attend the lodge meeting in *Rue Cadet* once a month."

"Ah, yes, your brethren. Maybe you'll meet some at the embassy."

"It could easily happen; some from the Ivory Coast are working in administration."

Edmond met Mamadou in the 19th arrondissement, where she lived, to accompany her to the meeting. She looked stunning. Her white dress fitted her like a second skin and emphasised her voluptuous figure.

They took a taxi to *102, Avenue Raymond Poincaré*, the Embassy of the Ivory Coast, not far away from the *Arc de Triomphe*. The road to the embassy was lined with acacia trees. It was a fine quarter, all with bright, distinguished old house fronts, with the famous flower shop *Gilles Pothier* on the opposite side, known for its exclusive flower arrangements.

The guard at the iron gate to the inner yard of the embassy checked their invitation card and IDs.
Entering the vestibule, they were welcomed by the ambassador. Ladies and gentlemen stood in groups engrossed in small talk.

Edmond glanced over the list of guests, and some names, titles and companies caught his eye:

Afrique Presse
TV5 Monde
Ministry of Agriculture of France
Representatives of Guinea, Mali, Burkina Faso, and Ghana, the neighbouring countries of the Ivory Coast.
Central Bank of West African States (BCEAO).
Managers of natural gas, diamond, and gold mining companies.

Edmond felt uncomfortable. He did not like those around whom he saw as exploiters and robbers of a country, of a continent, which they both, Edmond and Mamadou, loved.

When Mamadou and Edmond entered the anteroom, there was a brief silence, or so it seemed to him. Everyone looked at them, but all eyes were on Mamadou.
The ladies looked irritated and envious.
The men's eyes popped out of their heads.
They gawked. Edmond could read their horny thoughts.

Edmond shook hands with some he knew from business circles. He was, after all, the representative of a renowned French company in Germany.

The buffet reflected typical Ivorian cuisine: *Foufou*, a dish of mashed plantains and palm oil; *Attiéké*, like couscous and made from grated cassava. *Maafe*, meat in a peanut sauce, and Kedjenou, a spicy stew of chicken and vegetables, were offered. To his surprise and delight, he found Ivorian land snails grilled or eaten in sauce and *Alloco*, fried bananas.
To quench their thirst, they served *Bangui*, palm wine, ginger beer, and *Gnamakoudji*, pulped ginger with pineapple juice, lemon, and vanilla.

They started the event by playing the national anthem, "*Adieu les esclaves*" ("Farewell to the Slaves")
A band played gospel, jazz, salsa, and blues.
Edmond heard one of the indigenous languages: A theatre group showed a sketch in *Baoulé*, singers with captivating lightness, accompanied by their excellent drummers, played *Coupé-Décalé*.

Then the literary part started.

A Belgian lady recited a short story, a French student contributed with a chanson, and several African poets recited poems. Among them Daniel Maximin. After them, it was Edmond's turn. The audience seemed to be paying him particular attention.

He began to read; he knew the poem would be regarded as a provocation:

L'Afrique,
en forme d'assiette ovale,
une ardoise noire,
sur laquelle on écrit, on efface,
on étiquette à nouveau,
hier, aujourd'hui, demain,
un vaste terrain.

AFRICA
Africa, shaped as an oval plate,
a black slate,
written on, erased, labelled again,
yesterday, today, tomorrow,
a vast terrain.

Africa, shaped as an oval plate,
a table set with exotic food:
patata root,
rose harissa, aubergines,
bananas, coconut, beans,
okra, mango,
coriander and cilantro.
Served with lamb and tomato stew,
mutton, teff and foufou,
antelope and crocodile,
perch from the Nile.

Africa, shaped as a painting,
composed of earthy colours,
brown, red, terracotta,
framed with green and sienna,
blue and ochre,
amber.

Africa, shaped as a sculpture:
mountains, oasis, green pasture
rain forest, mangrove swamps,
lakes and savannas,
deserts, highlands.

Africa, shaped as luscious jewellery,
adorned with rubies and emeralds,
blue sapphires
and aquamarines,
precious diamonds.

Africa, shaped as an oval plate,
a black slate,
written on, erased, wiped off,
forgotten
today, tomorrow, rotten.

Africa, shaped as an oval plate,
high infant mortality rate,
Empty tables,
people deprived of food,
all exported, stolen.

Africa,
shaped as a painting,
composed with dark colours of death,

skin grey, festering purple,
the colour of blood mixing with the sod,
camouflage green, faint marine.

Africa, shaped as a sculpture,
exploited, bent, and deserted.
On the wall, the vulture
is watching his prey.
Towns vacated.

Africa,
shaped as luscious jewelleries,
violated, robbed,
diamonds are tears
and rubies are blood.

From Rutenga to Cape Town Bay
The train roars through the night,
crawling through the day,
stomps to the beat of the track bumps,
vibrating swivel plates and bolts responding,
the land's echo resounding
nadonga donga ...the melody.

There was a profound silence; some stared into the void, and then polite applause followed.

A representative of the cultural department came forward, looked at Edmond and turned to address the audience: "He loves Africa, he spoke to us from the heart, he is an ambassador of poetry."

Some elegantly dressed attendees returned to the buffet and resumed their casual conversations.

Edmond said to Mamadou: “I suppose they did not get it what I wanted to say.”

The ambassador joined them: Thanks for the poem. Highly appreciated.”

“Did you get what I wanted to say? Edmond growled. There was no response.

Some of the reps of the diamond industry stood within hearing distance.

“Africa is largely forgotten. Only natural resources are interesting. Not the people. We all bear responsibility.”

Mamadou put her hand on Edmond’s arm. She knew about his impulsiveness but also his engagement for Africa.

The group of mining companies’ representatives moved away. Edmond knew that they did not take him seriously.

Mamadou took his hand; she had tears in her eyes.

“Let’s go,” she said.

Writers' Groups

As if gathered
around a campfire,
in an adventurously daring way,
in joyful anticipation,
the flickering glow of a fire
on expectant faces.
It seems like a lifetime ago.

How lonely one must get,
to recognize all
what the poetry tree yields,
in its diversity?
Every work a single leaf.
Harvested ripe fruits.

Sharp edges that cast soft shadows,
that make the green blush.
Each leaf has an inscription.
Heart-shaped leaves,
beginning of novels,
final lines, reading samples,
long-sought-after rhymes
engraved into pages.

A gift for each of us,
breathed on ethereal paper,
each a unique work of art.

Detached we are,
as if we were an inclusion,
trapped in a drop of amber.

Here, in company, we fly free,
like a liberated bee,
we leave legible traces,
using lost words.
Deliver boldly unheard speeches,
backdate stories,
revitalize deleted words,
steer a sentence around corners.

We keep quiet during the week,
while on Sundays, we speak freely.
The laurel suits a few;
some are admitted into sacred halls.

We uphold our common vow,
of telling each other stories
until the end, impart,
ballads if necessary
share literary jewels.

Oh, my friends,
how I miss the promised land of poetry.
In the beginning, was the logos;
we are immortal only through words.

Consideration

Awaiting the spark,
that triggers the ignition,
I lie awake
and muse,
hope for inspiration,
divine or profane.

Paper in readiness,
sharpened the pencil.
I still write with lead,
but refuse the eraser,
this instrument of murder,
to delete innocent words,
I don't have the heart;
it causes too much pain
to throw nocturnal thoughts
into the bin.

Tracking

Scribes, scribblers, literature disciples
write poems, songs, and melodies,
according to their abilities
in Paris, Rome, and Naples.
They write of love and grief
of longing, joy, and fight
they always write
a piece of their own life.
On writers' tracks
to beauty, harmony, romance,
accompanied by boon and bane,
lust, transience, disdain.

Passion

Everybody hides a secret passion.
Questioned by a psychologist,
I would have to confess:
"It is books that caused this fervour.
Books generate
an almost erotic passion in me,
awake a wild craving.
The silky, soft feeling of paper,
the rustling of the sides,
captivate me,
I get hooked on the text,
the warming book in my hands,
carry it with me wherever I go,
a community of fate,
longing for more,
pledge eternal fidelity,
a treasure that has so much to say,
and I have so many questions.
He who reads lives,
he who lives loves.

4 am is poet's time.
I hear no bells chime,
only the gentle movement of leaves,
and the flap of moths' wings.

Absorbency

Wilted paper,
handmade,
offers itself, asks
with a questioning look,
for to be written on,
thirsting for ink,
as we are thirsty
for wine, for a drink,
spiritual sustenance.

Waxing Night Thoughts

Some people collect stamps
or bad experiences that emerge
and come forward
from behind black curtains.

I collect my own fantasies,
and try to mould them into something solid.
I let cascades of thoughts flow,
day and night,
create poems like chiselling a rough stone,
polishing its surface
and cut off useless excrescences.

Not just during the bright day,
but between 4 and 5 in the morning,
when dream streams turn into roaring waters,
into waterfalls
that thunder down to the valley,
only to calm down,
to spread out and then give birth to verses.

In the darkness of the night,
the blue ink of inspiration blurs
and I entrust my thoughts to the notepad,
because my handwriting
is as confused and abstruse
as my thoughts.

I call this ambivalent happiness
over rigid laws,
but it does not influence my poetry,
resembles more
the quietly flowing streams
in the *Spree Forest*,
that carry mysticism,
fairy tales and legends.

Ebb and Flow, Styx, and Acheron

The bistro “Emilio” on *Avenue Jean-Jaurès*, in the 19th arrondissement, was not an inviting bistro at first glance—a rather modern ‘*interieur*’ with neon lights—but strategically located between the music conservatory and the *Jean Jaurès Hospital*. It was a stop-over for people with short breaks. The menu was composed accordingly: salads of all kinds, croissants, crepes, soups, and sandwiches.
To give the bistro a Mediterranean flair, a fishnet with shells hung on the wall next to a colourful painting of the Italian coast.
I sat in a corner opposite the window, unfolded my newspaper, and waited for Amandine.
The *Toccata and Fugue in D minor BWV 565 by Johann Sebastian Bach* sounded from an open window of the *Conservatoire national supérieur de musique.*

The French love *Bach*.
Well, not all of them. The bistro owner closed the window with a decisive bang.

Amandine entered and took a seat next to me. She worked in the nearby hospital, and we met during her lunch break and when I had business in the neighbourhood.
She looked exhausted, with dark rings under her brown eyes.

“Two died last night in my ward after a hard battle. Hopes gone, all in vain.”

I listened to the organ music that drifted over to us and saw in my mind the keys of the lower row of ivories moving in front of me as if moved by an invisible hand because the organist activated them with his feet. The beginning of the piece was played with two fingers on the upper row.

The bistro owner put a *Caprese* on the table: Mozzarella, tomatoes, basil, and olive oil like a promising prelude.

"A greeting from the kitchen; tell me how you find it," he said. We smiled in gratitude.

"I hope to be an organist when I am reborn."

"Why?" Amandine asked.

"Because I have been musically untalented since childhood, I have no clue about music. I have always admired *Bach, Mozart, Handel, Verdi, and Beethoven, as well as* their performers. Those skilful fingers and feet mastering the organ, violinists playing sweeping lines from low strings to high, and pianists' virtuosity. I loved coffee house music, chansons, the discreet piano in hotel lobbies, and concerts, though I could not read or understand notes or play an instrument. A chip is missing."

"You rave for music, and at the same time, you mourn not having this talent."

"Why can creation not be more perfect? Why is the world divided into privileged and unprivileged? Talented and untalented? Yes, I find it sad, a mental handicap, a lack of intellect, a flawed construction.

"That's not true, you write poetry that touches people."

"Nobody reads poetry."

"Don't say that."

During their break, students from the conservatory crossed the street and entered the bistro in a big wave.
The students had enraptured faces and looked almost captivated, as if in another sphere. Delicate young ladies, detached young men.

"Look at their hands, Amandine."

Their hands were delicate, fragile, agile, and virtuosic, accustomed to holding and playing an instrument. Light-footed and floating were those who studied dance. From their movements, I guessed they were dancers, porcelain dolls performing pirouettes on tiptoe. Dying swans, I thought and had to laugh.

I overheard a group of three students talking about their vocal studies. Faces with small, red-lipped mouths, their voices sounded like birdsong accompanied by a student's baritone.

And I saw all these gifted people, the pride of their parents, and me, next to them, an untalented old cripple who had not stood out as a loser only because of his shrewdness.

As if in defiance, the bistro owner turned on his music. *Paolo Conte* sang: ... *chi bum, chi bum. It's wonderful. It was* followed by *Andrea Bocelli's 'I Love You Tender'*.
The students took no notice.

The flow to the bistro reversed into an ebb back to the conservatory. Soon, the bistro emptied.

Amandine looked at her watch, then at me, and said:

life is an adieu
to my moribund I go
to wait at Styx's shore

"Oh, one of your haiku", I responded admiringly.

"Phone me this evening and write a poem." She waved goodbye and left. I ordered a double espresso.

The bistro owner opened the window again.
From a distance, I heard violin melodies.
A loud, rushed staccato of hard-soled shoes sounded in the street.

I heard a shot followed by a second one. Soon, the blue lights of police cars and an ambulance approached.

The two men playing cards at the neighbouring table stopped their game and went to the window, and the owner came from behind the bar.
Someone was lying face down on the other side of the avenue.
Men in white coats ran to the victim, examined him, and shook their heads.

It reminded me of the Lutheran hymn "In the Midst of Life we are in Death".
Someone played the Toccata and Fugue in D-Minor again.

A man with a silver-grey artist's mane closed the conservatory window from which the toccata hovered over the street and cut the piece in the middle.

I pulled a wrinkled piece of paper from my pocket, smoothened it out, went through the text and made a few changes:

STYX and ACHERON
A dreamland wide and lush
borders reality lands,
cold, hard, and harsh.
Wolves howl in the vast expanse,
the cries of ravens shrill.
Birds gather in a bush,
uncertainty beyond the hill.

A name written on a shard,
a name we cannot read,
it might be our own.
Who knows?
Maybe Charon, the ferryman of death
can tell
who offers a crossing over to Hades.

From far sounds the poor sinner's bell,
a knell
we heard too often, a hundred times.
We count the chimes
of towers in the distance,
hear chorales, choirs, chants.

We count our remaining days.
But in vain.
We end unsuccessfully, strand,
face unknown borders
on unpredictable horizons,
skylines which change their colours,

daily,
from silver to grey,
from azure to dead black
from crimson to blood red.

Morphology
I awoke from a dream
and had a book in my hand,
which fell from a pile
next to my head.
I left the hand where it is -
on the book -
and hoped that the knowledge,
the skills,
the feelings, the poetic art,
will seep through the arm
to my heart,
fills it with images, good vibes,
thoughts' green meads.

At night, I hear knocking noises,
I notice with relief,
it is only my heart that beats.

Lost Poem

I am desperately looking for a poem text,
composed with clearly visible letters,
and can no longer find it,
it no longer exists.
I am perplexed.
It stood before my eyes all night in my dreams.
I'll have to reinvent it, it seems.
It faded away with the rising of the sun,
like misty ghosts
that shy away from daylight,
taking away what I have done.

Displaced Language

In the beginning
I had only one language.
Objects, feelings,
colours and dreams,
were enclosed in it
like flies
in a piece of amber.

At the age of four
a second one was added;
imposed,
my father loved the French.
His own experience taught him
to have several tongues
and a handful of passports,
not to run the risk to be
trapped, held hostage
by hostile regimes
as it happened to him once.

Decades ago
I learned my first English words.
Now, I have been writing for five years,
actively,
but still unable to express me
as I wished I could, satisfactorily,
not to inflict pain
on the audience.

I do not speak correctly,
bit broken, with an appalling accent,
write by consulting dictionaries,
call the other languages
enemy languages.
The reason,
a serious one:
these languages
are gradually
killing my mother tongue.

You become a writer
by writing patiently, arduously,
without ever losing faith
in what you write.

I write by the light of the moon,
the full moon, in the night,
under the fertile moonlight,
sentences take shape.
They circle around me,
get a rhythm, rhymes,
a melody, become poems.

Memory refuses to recall moments
in which I have lost part of my life.
I lost my ethnicity in a cold January,
a life of strife.
I would have written anywhere
where I would have settled
and in the language of that place.

I did not choose a language.
They came to me by fate,
by chance, by circumstances,
they opened a gate
to other spheres.
To be an emigrant is a challenge,
a wanderer between worlds
and words.

Genesis of Poems

The evening sun sinks weak and weary,
his hand is reaching for a page,
he hesitates, is dreamy,
pushes the paper away
to the edge of the table.

Then he considers tensely,
closes his eyes,
and words, lines, a lost dream fragment,
appear
as if on a continuous neon sign band.

He pulls the blank page towards him,
ponders again, hesitates for a moment,
then he sets his pen firmly and clearly
on the empty rectangle sheet,
takes a sip of red wine,
to fertilise his thoughts,
at least to ignite, accelerate,
to spur them on.

The first line is created,
a triplet emerges,
where in the stanza, the first line
is repeated in the fourth and seventh,
and the second in the last, the eighth.
Two rhymes, the limit,
as in *Rimbaud*'s poem
"The Stolen Heart",

Where does the inspiration come from?
Where come all the poems from
since time immemorial?

Are they dreams during the night?
Is it the candlelight,
the light of the sun or the stars
memoirs,
the expanse of the taiga,
the haze of the tundra,
the mystery of dark forests,
the sound of the sea?

It is the embellishment
of ancient, submerged fantasies,
stories, fables, inventions,
expanded, the thread spun on,
in whimsical turns.

Basically,
everything is a human invention,
finely spun yarn
beautiful illusions,
fears stirred up
or originating from them.
Deriving from gatherings
around campfires on desert nights.
adventures in misty Nordic forests,
fields full of aurochs, wolves, and bears.

Minds fed by fear, suspicion,
superstition,
fear of the unknown,

to which they attributed divine qualities,
to explain the reasons for floods,
volcanic eruptions,
storms and weather, devastations,
as the wrath of the gods,
who became human-like,
to make their own infinite powerlessness,
nothingness and tininess bearable.
This gave rise to poems and stories
up to our days.

Between Day and Dream

4.30 a.m. The night is gone (for me)
but the creativity tap is open
and a poem flows gently.
I had a dream
that I travelled the Silk Road,
rested in a desert,
took the Incense Route
milked the *olibanum* tree
in a barren, stony area,
cut into its bark, causing it injuries,
collected tree sap, frankincense,
harvested Allah's tears.
I drank black tea,
with a Sheikh in his tent
not far blossomed the desert rose
its scent mixed with the fragrance
of myrrh and incense.

Flew over the sea
and sat with an indigenous,
over a pipe of tobacco;
he mourned the loss of his culture,
rolled down by strangers from far
who stole their gold,
the tears of their gods.

Met a friendly black man
who, in his subconscious,
remembered the rainforests

in Africa, the vast savannahs,
and counted his scars
and those of his fellowmen
caused by slave traders.

And in Asia, the sons of gods
built forbidden cities,
temples, sacred realms,
to be godlike because they were,
subconsciously, fallen, or outcast angels.
Wanted to revive the divine,
reactivate, renew the godlike.

I drank tea with the monks,
tea with the water drops
from the lotus blossoms,
hear the two-string fiddle,
the *dan-tam* lute, the bamboo flute.
They establish a connection
between here and there
the caves under the shore,
where dragons wait for centuries
to defend them, give eternal life,
provide strength.

Passing poetry

Only twenty minutes from *Grand Moulins de Paris*, where I worked, and in walking distance of *Place de la Bastille* is the *Boulevard de Ménilmontant*, which runs alongside the famous Parisian graveyard.
Opposite the yellow wall of the cemetery *Père Lachaise* is a café with the fitting name *La Purgatoire.* At its right, the shop of an undertaker - *Lutèce.* The road is dotted with funeral homes and undertakers, the marketplace of transience.
An alley with trees in front of a row of houses alleviates the permanence of death.

After a long working day, I have always enjoyed resting in this quiet part of Paris. I like to sit in a cosy café, where people have their coffee or a meal, read their newspapers or a book, or engage in a conversation.

I push the café door open to Jacques Brel's **Il y a** resounding from a CD player.

Over the past months, I have noticed an old man who leaned over a heap of paper and wrote. Pausing from time to time, he looked over to the walls of the cemetery until he returned to his notes. He had a white beard, glasses, and a black velvety jacket. A rolled cigarette dangled from his lower lip. His hands looked rough and worn.

Without having ordered, a double espresso was put in front of me by Maëlys, the owner. I liked her friendly face and the gentle, accidental touch of her hand when she served the coffee.

I felt she liked me, too. She was the type of woman who made you write love letters or poems.

I asked her discretely who the old man was. She bowed and whispered, “He is a poet, Monsieur Jean-Claude Laferre. He lives down the road. He spends most of his time here. I do not mind; my café seems to be his second home.”

I went through my files, as I had to prepare a report for the chairman of my company and did not notice when the old poet left.

Days later, I saw him again sitting in a corner before his notes. I passed by his desk, said Bonsoir, which he returned without looking up. “I love poems”, I said, “I tried to write a few, but I presume I am ungifted.”

“Everybody can write poems”, he said.

He looked up and saw my questioning glance.
“Everybody is creative from birth on. You have to allow your creativity to emerge. I presume you are a manager. Your mind is buried by facts and figures, appointments, and duties. There is little place for creativity. Oh well, you might be creative in your job. That is all right; that is also a form of creativity.”

“Can you show me one of your poems?”

“Sit down”, he said. He pushed a piece of paper over to me.

I read:

Late Harvest Moon

Through a greenish curtain shot a spark.
Now it is gone. What's bothering my heart?
Colourful summer burned to the ground,
sun-kissed in golden deaths.
A withered mound of humus found
to pave the path for flora's birth.
How may we walk so lost in thoughts
through tawny meadows' band?
Over us, free, untamed across
wide clouds of light expand.
And all around the pale, discoloured world
in contemplative farewell stillness,
as if in every leaf impressed
a holy fate is silently fulfilled.

As he rolled another cigarette, I asked him:

"What do you see as the meaning of poetry? Hanging word cloths on thought lines?
To construct artificial rhymes, to give sense to verses, to put melancholy on paper, or to torment others with one's thoughts?"

"I see you have not understood poetry. Why does someone write - a journalist, an analyst, a philosopher? To put a thesis on the wall? To manifest something? No, they have a story to tell; they "manufactured" a written piece.
I was a stonemason and sculptor; I chiselled statues and head-stones from rough material until I created something nearly perfect for my eye. I do the same when I write a poem, which is challenging. I worked with marble, travertine, sand- and lime-

stone. Now I can sculpt word by word on paper, having exchanged the hammer and chisel with the pen."

Months later, I revisited the café. Maëlys put my espresso in front of me.
"I missed you", she said.
"Great to be missed, especially by a beautiful lady", I said.
"You old charmer", she responded.

Maëlys served a customer in the back of the café. When she passed my table, she said:
"The poet died two weeks ago."

She pointed to his table. There stood a vase with a few chrysanthemums and some sheets of paper.
"A memorial for him. His favourite flowers and some of his poems."
"I presume he was not buried over there?" I nodded to the cemetery opposite.
"No", Maëlys said, "very few poets are buried in Père Lachaise; poets are transitory, as are their poems."
Somebody entered the café.
When the door opened, a piece of paper with one of the poems lifted and flew out of the door, tumbled, made a jump, turned in the air, slid over the road and flew over the wall of Père Lachaise…
On my way to my car, I passed the window of the neighbouring funeral company. An epitaph was displayed in the window:

Man, become essential:
For, when this world is gone/
All accident is past/
The essence still lives on.

Angelus Silesius

Story Fabric, Woven Moon Gaze

A song hovers like falling leaves.
Weathered from clusters of high trees,
sheaves waft on far-stretched fields.
The many thoughts got sharded,
It died the last will, isolated.
I braided poem words
into a yellow-gold plait.
Sunken memories cause a chill.
Unboundedness streams
and drowns in loneliness.
In a staggering flight
I see a coal-black bird
in the sun-warm, silver-white sky.
Rust-red sunset on the horizon.
Against the heaven rising
stands a delicate curved line,
arcing the sphere
over earth's confine
and the scream rolling sea.

Pen in hand,
the eye turned inwards.
I make a journey
into the depth of language.
Collect the words that faded in pain,
moistened by bitterly wrenched tears,
harshly laughed at taunted fears,
overriding the burning embers
of my blood's boil stream;

the flaring blaze of my fantasy -
my heart cinders.

Shrieks fall into abysmal nights,
white chrysanthemums,
the remnants of lightheartedness
lose their petals.

Poets' Quest

At dusk,
when sunset descends,
I thought it was time
to proceed to *Rue de Librairie*
with its belle epoque facades
opposite the *Hôtel de la Raymondie*.
For a moment, I paused
in front of *Rimbaud*,
before I climbed up *Rue de Faubourg*,
a tree-lined alley with cobblestones.

I was greeted with an embrace.
There was something balmy
and springlike in the atmosphere,
a buoyant suspense.
Like moments
before the conductor's baton is raised,
buzzing sounds of tuned instruments.
Then silence and expectation,
the holding of the breath,
followed by a relaxation

After I had recited my poems,
not knowing whether they understood
what I meant and had read,
or been bored,
a question was asked by a lady
from the audience,
(she was attractive,

exuded old-fashioned elegance,
her voice sounded
like the bells of *St. Sulpice*):

"Why are your poems so triste,
horrible, terrifying, full of weariness,
full of hopelessness?"

"The present hurts, and the past festers
like an abscess of suffering,
dark clouds gather
as if caught on a mountain's edge,
prevented to float on,
hovering away,
but they transform into words
and rain down on the slopes,
turn into rivulets that make stones speak
without moving them.

Shadows become letters and line up,
verbatim, sentence by sentence,
sometimes admonishing,
sometimes threatening
or just hanging their heads in tears
waiting for a ray of hope as
sunlight that illuminates the fields,
sends words as fleeting signs
like restless flocks of swallows
in the sombre wild vines,
chubby cumulus clouds
drift across the blue sky.
A respite is granted to us,
a break, a deceptive hope."

From there, these poems emerge,
grow to strength, gain length,
are abridged, tweaked,
tilted and turned
until they stand on solid ground,
verses to make strings sound,
to lead out of despair,
to pour the daybreak into hearts.
As written manifestos
that not all is lost.

The Cosmos of a Poet

Surrounded by thorny hedges
of a forbidding repellent world
behind a blackthorn hedgerow
with the entangled wool of sheep
white signs they bestow
like ethereal notes that sigh and weep.

A walk through blind alleys,
a knot garden of words
of a garrulous world,
a maze of sentences,
grown like wild jungle lianas,
like wild blackberries.

Plankton fishing in lyric oceans,
casting his net to catch emotions
or sow thoughts on fertile humus:
Spreads seeds of colourful flowers
plucks them, binds them into bouquets,
Writes odes and ballads, sonnets.

To weave wreaths of praise and glory
into an epitaph or elegy
the poet collects blossoms and leaves,
the song of birds, the sound of the waves,
gives them form and name,
chiselled from rough stones,
into stanzas, verses, epigrams.

Commemoration

I hold a book of poems in my hand,
read verse after verse,
verses that send
my thoughts, feelings,
and inward peace.

The poets, dead, long before time,
passed by, fell asleep dreamily,
hear and feel my readings,
gently, metaphysically,
lift themselves from their graves
and listen to my quiet recitation,
thank with a smile, ethereally sigh,
that they are remembered
and thus, made immortal,
their poetry is not rendered
in vain.

Dilemma of a Quadrilingual

With a mixture of remembrance
and nostalgia
I am aware of a phenomenon
which we call
the confusion of tongues,
a language plethora
that we owe
to the times of *Babylon*:
This exile lingo:
The *emigranto*,
that inimitable mélange
with trace elements
of indigenous dialects and accents
plus other bits and pieces
of my countries of transit.
To quote a Viennese cabaret artist:
I am a hell of a fix
while I German and English fine mix.

Writing Contest

"I will not eat a single hazelnut,
unless you are by my side..."

a Black Sea folk song

Akçay and his wife Semra lived in the province of *Giresun* on the Turkish Black Sea Coast, in a landscape blessed with lakes and rivers, where forests and pastures cover the mountainous region.

When their hazelnut groves yielded less and less, and they were in danger of having to sell their land to the larger plantations, Akçay decided to take a job in Germany.
Semra was sad, but it comforted her that he planned to stay only a year. Their wider family had a history of work migration, with cousins who had worked in *Frankfurt,*
Dortmund, or *Ludwigshafen*.

On the way to the airport in *Ankara*, in his cousin's car, Akçay promised to write Semra a letter at least every month. Semra promised it too, even though she could hardly write. But cousin Feridun knew a letter writer in a neighbouring village who could write a flawless and faultless letter either upon dictation or by using the information, facts, ideas, and news provided by his clients, which he would put into a properly written, elegant, and appealing form. He knew what people wanted to read and how to edit and present it in a digestible form. Be it good news or bad news. He even had a typewriter, albeit a rickety one.

Akçay's writing skills were limited, and so was his vocabulary, which was defined by and confined to the radius of his activities, namely herding, milking their goats, caring for their nut groves, working occasionally as a fitter in his old uncle's workshop, or sitting on the forest slope dreaming and looking over the Anatolian countryside.

Akçay regretted his limited writing skills because it prevented him from competing in a successful nut business.
He remembered that the apostle Paul had written letters to the Galatians. The Galatians had been at home in his part of the country, far away from their Celtic homeland. Paul was able to write letters long before Muhammad wrote the *Quran*, the Prophet be praised.

It was a long journey from *Giresun* to *Ankara*—more than a six-hour drive. They stayed silent during the journey. There was not a lot to be said. Akçay embraced the landscape, which he would not see for a while. They crossed the clean, well-cared-for towns of *Ordu, Ünye, and Corum* with their multitude of shops, using the wide, good roads until they arrived at the modern airport in the outskirts of *Ankara.*

He had only a small cardboard suitcase that held the bare necessities. His wife and cousin wished him a safe journey before he disappeared behind the security area.

The *Corendon Airlines* flight from *Ankara* *to Düsseldorf* landed on time.
On board, people wore faces in which he saw traces of melancholy, or which were full of tense expectations like his. Others, in dark suits, busily reaching for their mobile phones as soon as they landed.
Ergün, a compatriot from a town neighbouring his village who

had gotten him the job, picked him up at the airport and drove him to the factory worker's home. It was clean and tidy. Ergün had, as a welcome, prepared sheep's cheese and *gözleme*, stuffed flatbread, and *dolmas*.

Ergün had achieved something. He proudly reported that he had become a foreman in the factory, chairman of the *IG Metall* trade union in his district, and writer for the local Turkish newspaper.
His car was an upmarket Audi.

Akçay told Ergün about his promise to write a letter to his wife every month.
Downplaying his inability, he said: "Could you help me? I have no imagination. I have problems with composing a letter."

"We will see, I will help you", promised Ergün.

Weeks passed, and Akçay scribbled words on a piece of paper: Arrived well, good accommodation, good colleagues, good money. Good country. Cold.

He put the letter into an envelope and struggled with writing the address. He carefully copied the letters from a piece of paper, got a stamp and threw the letter into the yellow post box.
After two weeks, a neatly typed letter from Semra arrived:

Dearest Akçay,
how pleasant it was to hold the letter in my hand that you held in yours. It was as if our hands were touching each other. I kissed the letter.
It made me happy, and I showed it to the seagulls that hover lonely over the coast and miss you too. As I do.

I love you with all my heart.

Akçay was amazed. He had never heard Semra expressing herself like that.
He felt bad when he thought about the scanty words in his letter. He asked Ergün to write something appropriate as a response because, he repeated, he had no imagination, but his wife was very clever and poetic.

"And she can type, all respect," Ergün said.

Ergün drafted a letter. He noticed that Akçay had difficulty reading and read the letter to him:
Your words sent the fragrance of the pine trees of our mountains, and when you mention the seagulls, I see the blue sea in front of me......

"Very nice, I couldn't have said it better myself," Akçay smiled and said: "Please add that there's a Turkish supermarket here and a meeting place where I can play cards with the country-men. And that I go to the mosque every Friday and pray for her. It's cold for September, but the accommodation is warm."

Ergün said, "All right, but it sounds so matter of fact. I will write that you enjoy the strong Turkish coffee here, ... *my body withers if I don't drink coffee, just as my soul withers without you...*
Weeks later, another letter waited for him which the postman left in the caretaker's office in the worker's home.

Dearest Akçay,
I see you are in good hands. Thanks be to Allah.
I send you the warmth of my hands, the mildness of our coast, and the rays of the sun that ripened our hazelnuts.

For the first time after many years, we have a good harvest.
We missed you at harvest time, but Feridun and his wife
Güzel helped me.
The hazelnuts are round and brown. You did right to drive the goats into the grove, they eat the weeds and fertilise the ground.

It is so peaceful,
the mountain slopes fall gently,
my heart is full of joy,
the paths
take my steps lightly.

On the water, wild geese, and ducks.
In the sky, black kites, and sparrow hawks.
The sun shines on the hazel trees
which sway in the mild breeze.

The market is full and lively,
loaded with fruits in all colours
offers in abundance,
yellow butter
with its grassy, rich taste,
sweet cicely,
bread, round and heavy
spread with pepper paste.

I know I ignite homesickness
but the time to your return gets less.

Akçay met Ergün in a coffee house near the factory. The weather was autumnal, foggy, and grey, dominated by a metallic stench and a strong smell of fumes.
He was surrounded by the sound of cars, the humming crowds in the streets, the grinding of heavy equipment, and church bell

chimes that cut through the mist. An environment far removed from the one he was accustomed to.
He sighed and showed Ergün Semra's letter. Erdün smiled.
A tram drove by with squealing wheels, and an ambulance with blue lights.

Akçay felt lonely. The early darkness hit his mind. He had night shifts and slept during the day. This never-ending darkness gripped his heart.

Ergün invited him to join him with friends on Sunday.

"When the stomach is full of things from home, the world looks different," Ergün said with an encouraging smile.
He promised that there would be *Etli Ekmek*, a thin, crispy flatbread topped with ground beef and finely chopped onions, tomatoes, and peppers, lamb stew, and *baklava* as dessert. And, of course, *raki* to help with digestion.

A factory siren sounded nearby, and the container crane signals of the *Duisburg* inland port could be heard from afar.

Ergün offered to write a few lines to Semra and post the letter to save Akçay the trip to the post office.

Akçay gave Ergün a photo of him with his colleagues in front of modern tool machines in a factory hall and a photo of him with friends at a meal and asked Ergün to put them in the envelope with the letter.

Ergün wrote:

I would like to take the brush
and dip it into the blueness of the sea
into the fields of carnations and asters
to paint the dark walls in light colours
to brighten the greyness of a cold land,
and ease my pain
with the wild-growing mint,
lavender and lemon balm leaves.

I smell the fragrance, perceive it
when I think of it.
I hear the music of the tambour lute,
fiddle, zither, violin, flute,
and küdüm drum and harp,
to forget the pounding sound of the machinery,
the metallic cacophonous noise of the industry.

Two weeks later, a letter arrived with some colourful stamps artistically arranged on a blue envelope:

Dearest Akçay,

The harvest has brought good coin
for the hazelnuts so brown.
First cranes and storks arrived,
the farmers plough their land,
winter raises its hand
beckons from afar.

A nightingale sings
and spreads joy and lore,
yet the days grow shorter
and my patience even more.

The leaves change colour
as if taken from a paint box,
with chestnut and beech
pomegranates in big numbers.

Soon, the leaves will fall again
and the wind will churn.
The year is ending
next year will bring your return.

I stick coloured stamps
like autumn leaves,
the fifteen Kuruş stamp in pink,
thirty Kuruş stamp in forget-me-not blue
sixty Kuruş stamps in pistachio green
on my sea-blue envelope
and send you the expanse of the Black Sea,
the flapping wings of herons and flamingos.

Ergün and Çalışkan wrote prose and poetry, and it turned out to be a competition between two writers who had never met.

But everybody was happy and enjoyed it. The couple with the alleged talent and profundity of each other, the well-wrapped-up news, the tradition of presentation of stories and poetry.

Soon, it turned August and, with it, the approaching nut harvest. Akçay prepared for his return journey.
He had earned good money. He said goodbye to his colleagues, and a weight fell from his heart when he left the austere area, the frightening buildings, the town, and the walls behind, the

monotonous noise day and night, the roar and stench of the factories and the port.
Semra and Feridun picked him up at *Ankara Esenboğa Airport*.

He had a lot to tell. Semra noticed that his stories had become prose, containing more and new words that he had never used before. Semra gave her report on everyday things that had happened in the family, in their mountain village.

The familiar landscape whizzed past them. They stopped at a small grocery to drink an *ayran*, drove through busy streets lined with shops which sold copper pitchers and carpets, passed a row of taxi minibuses, the stands of orange sellers, saw old men drinking tea and having a chat or idling outside the coffee shops. They passed fish stalls selling mackerel, lamprey eel, and turbot. He was home again.

Semra mentioned the poems Akçay had sent her, and she laughed.

"And I thought you had gone among the poets despite your back-breaking work.
But I have learned something; I realised what kind of world I miss if you can't read and write well. It's a challenge. I heard of emigrants whose fate forced them to write in another language, practically from one day to the other, and how they struggled but finally succeeded.

I read the short stories by *Rafik Schami.* He fled from Syria to Germany, and now he writes successfully in German..... and I started writing poetry."

"What?" Akçay looked at her with wide eyes.

“Here, listen”, she said:

On the terrace by the sea
I spread the blossoms of jasmine
to dry.
The day is ending,
and with it, the harvesting
I bring the yield home.
The night rises, is reborn.”

Akçay had tears in his eyes.

“It reminds me of classes in our village school,” he said,” when the teacher read the poems of the Turkic peoples. I still remember the rhyme and rhythm.
I admit, I got textbooks, or rather Ergün gave me some after he realised my struggle with the language, and I learned in my free time.
Ergün wrote poetry and created pleasant letters in my stead. I would only have written about the greyness and the monotony of the work and the everyday loneliness and boredom, but the books opened a new world for me, spurred me on.”

Their village appeared on the horizon. Friends and relatives were waiting for him when he arrived and welcomed him. He was served coffee and bread and *İmam bayıldı,*stuffed eggplant.

The following day, Akçay took his baskets and went to the hazelnut grove to greet his hazelnut bushes and to start the harvest.

A poem arose in his mind:

Beige-brown is the hazelnut,
green-brown the mountain range.
Homely, high-growing bushes
with roundish, rough leaves,
the dust of your yellow catkins
powders the air,
a bee pasture in spring.

Word Forge

Many words we utter.
They fall into shafts,
into streams, into the gutter.
Prudently
we let them pass through a sieve,
where they may gain weight
or fly forth like birds' feathers,
thoughtlessly spoken
they shatter like glass,
fall into a bottomless pit,
seep into the mud.

By a lightning of thought
they flash, appear in a dash,
fall silent,
find form through type cases,
and printing presses
under the smell of printing inks,
or are on galley proofs,
form headlines, word formations,
prints,
birthday cards, invitations,
posters, newspapers, art,
literary texts, even poems -
then fade away and escape
to be remembered,
to be reborn again.

The last word has not yet been spoken.

The Sorceress of Endor

She sits there, the nethermancer,
with a wry, suspicious gaze,
makes the spinning wheel hum,
let the woollen thread run
through her scrawny hands.
She offers a glimpse into the future,
seductively, into the netherworld,
behind my fading life's curvature.

I refuse, it could be bad news,
an unwanted reflection.
She nods her head,
affirms my hesitation,
my reluctance, my fear of the future,
my fear of the inevitable
lurking behind the final curtain,
for the final performance,
if I can still walk the distance;
she cuts the problem bread
with the knife of finality.

What's the use of making plans,
filling the days in vain?
She lifts the finger and murmurs:
"Sort out your piles of books,
some still unread,
organise your legacy",
she says bleary-eyed, wiseacred,
"take the burden off other shoulders,

sift through your possessions
and dispose of them,
fill black plastic bags,
dump them or give them away.

None of your poems was ever printed,
and will not be printed, be assured,
so it is no loss for mankind,
you will quickly be forgotten,
your piles of poetry notes
and sheets full of poems
will be offered to the fire,
to give the world some fleeting warmth.

Death of a Poet

Homage to *Hans Magnus Enzensberger*

A voice has fallen silent,
a loud, critical, and clear voice.
His books, novels, and poems
have found an end.
A chapter has been closed.

He is now, laurel-wreathed,
in the poets' Hall of Fame,
in the eternal shadow realm
of a distant pantheon.
The award-winning "utopia"
still reverberates
in consistent lower case,
which begins like this:

"*The day rises with great power*
puts its claws through the clouds....."

Germany's foremost poet
of the postwar period,
a provocative essayist,
a highly influential editor
an intellectual multi-talent.
a solitaire
among poets and thinkers.

Enzensberger embodied
the freedom of thought and opinion,

accompanied the history of Germany,
whose founding he witnessed
as a twenty-year-old
in the ruins of a destroyed country.

Was a founder member of Group 47,
an orientation figure for the 1968 movement.
His book of poems,
"*Defence of the Wolves Against the Lambs*",
swept like a whirlwind
into the petit-bourgeois comfort of the fifties.

Grass and *Böll* lined his path.
And the French Enlightenment thinker
Denis Diderot,
whose work he translated into German.

Enzensberger's poems are
political or provocative,
of stunning beauty,
and crafted brilliantly.
To give some impression
I will provide you with my translation:

into the reading book
for the upper secondary school
do not read odes, my son, read the timetables:
they are more precise. roll up the sea charts
before it is too late. be vigilant, do not sing.
the day comes when they nail lists to the gate
again, and paint secret signs on the naysayers' chests.
learn walking in disguise, learn more than I did:
to change the district, the passport, and the face.

be ready for the little betrayal,
the daily dirty escape. useful
are the encyclicals to light a fire,
the manifestos: to wrap butter and salt
for the defenceless. anger and patience are necessary
to blow into the lungs of power
the fine, deadly dust, ground
by those who have learned a lot,
who are accurate, thanks to you.

A lot of his poems were at the time a beacon.
Now, they are a piece of history.
being an opponent of nuclear weapons,
an opponent of rearmament, he said:
I am quite happy to be asynchronous...

Hans Magnus Enzensberger
wants his poems to be understood
like inscriptions, posters, leaflets,
carved into a wall, pasted onto a wall,
distributed in front of a wall;
they should not fade away in space,
in the ears of the one, patient reader,
but be in the eyes of many,
especially of the impatient,
they should stand and live,
should be like a newspaper ad,
a poster on an advertising pillar,
a writing in the sky.

They should be messages,
here and now,
for all of us.

Translator or Traitor?

Asked whether I have
favourite words,
a literal preference:
I chose 'Friendship' and 'Peace'.
They dropped out of fashion
seeing the unpeaceful
and unfriendly world around us.
I found and find them in lyrics.

I write in four languages
play with words, expressions.
And I love poetry,
it is my passion, a deep love, an addiction
which makes life bearable, lighter,
not only for me.
I feel,
it is a therapy to console and heal.

With poets from all over this earth
I keep close contact, with my friends,
and help them to transport
their verses, their feelings
into languages other than their own,
and realise how hard it can be
to maintain meaning and tone.
One does not say lightly
that a translation
is a kiss through a veil.
I read the first lines

to see if the text resonates with me,
look forward to reading more,
do a quick translation,
a framework, then the fine-tuning,
start to chisel like a sculptor.

Some languages are terse,
some flowery,
some do not rhyme easily,
some have long words,
or words are monosyllabic
I ponder to find the right word
like on piano ivories, the right sound
or the strings of a harp.

Sometimes, the right word
comes to the surface by chance,
when I wake up at four,
suddenly, a poem arises.
I hasten to write it down
not to forget the words,
go to the kitchen,
brew a coffee to wake me up,
to start the day and stroke my cat.

I sit until late in the night
to get the text and the stanzas right.
I take the poet's place,
stand in his shoes,
try to look through his eyes,
gaze into his secret realms,
over borders, bridges, and hills,
I tap like on fine porcelain

to test the sound,
the purity of tone.

The Italians say:
The *Traduttore*, the translator
is always a *Traditore*, a Traitor.
I deny that outright.
I keep the poem entrusted to me
like a piece of ancient bone china
which speaks to me.
And each stanza
is carefully turned, weighted,
viewed from all angles
to find a twin
perfect in all its limbs.

Stanzas in a city of light

Edmond had been busy with a project that required extensive travel outside Paris for the last few weeks.

And no time for poetry, his passion.

The late morning was filled with doing his shopping at the neighbouring baker and the butcher and buying a packet of *Macarons*.
He intended to see his friends in the *'Club Literaire'*.

The washing machine was filled, and he pressed the button.
To get ready for the evening, he rooted through his cupboard.
The choice was not extensive. His favourite colour was black, and he selected black trousers, a black shirt, and a black jacket.
He smiled when he pulled a black T-shirt from a shelf with the imprint "Poetry is sexy."

Edmond phoned Mamadou Assamoua, the organizer of the club events. She was a friend in a double sense—a poet and a woman. Although she was ten years older than Edmond, he felt inspired and secure in her presence, which he had been deprived of during the last few weeks. She was from the Ivory Coast.

„I thought you had abandoned me", she said.

„How could I? I would be lost", confessed Edmond. „I was busy jobwise. Is the club open?"

„No, but the bistro is."

When he went down the staircase, his footsteps echoed in the hallway, and when he passed the concierge, she said to Edmond: "You did not put your waste in the appropriate bin. We have waste separation here."

He answered with a 'hasty' haiku:

on the eve of World War III
waste separation - paramount
false priorities

Edmond left the house and a perplexed concierge behind.

He intended to spread the haiku virus wherever he was, but this served as an arrow shot in the direction of the concierge, a poetic weapon.

For him, the streets after sunset were like spines of books of unknown content; illuminated windows appeared like pages, and behind house fronts, multiple fates developed, smouldered, and unfolded and were sources for prose and poetry. He observed his surroundings with a watchful eye to get inspiration for his poetry and took in the impulses that reached him. Cafes and bistros were the cruising places for him.

The traffic was still busy, but rush hour was ending. He took the metro to the 11th arrondissement, where the *'Club Littéraire'* was located.

For Edmond, the bistro on the ground floor was a school and stage, and at the same time, it had friends and writers who were known and emerging. Writers met here in a modernist '*arcadia*' in a historic building dating back to the French Revolution. It had been the abode of a Jacobin club.

As buildings in Paris exude and ooze history, a city built on six million dead, one could be confident that no dull thoughts were hatched under this roof but that the era of the 'Enlightenment' was omnipresent.

The bistro's glass front faced the street, and passers-by could see the motley mix of patrons inside or the few customers outside who had the resilience to sit at the round tables in front of the establishment on a chilly October night.
When he passed the outdoor area, he heard a journalist interviewing an elderly gentleman.
The man's accent sounded Austrian, even though he spoke fluent and immaculate French. Edmond recognised *Georg Stefan Troller*, a filmmaker and writer, a Jewish émigré to Paris after his family had to leave their home in Vienna in 1938.

He overheard fragments of their dialogue:
"When I was a television correspondent, I met *Somerset Maugham.* During the interview, he pulled a booklet from his jacket and quoted a poem by *Goethe* in fluent German. He had studied in *Heidelberg*……

The gods give everything, the infinite ones,
To their beloved, completely,
Every pleasure, the infinite ones,
Every suffering, the infinite ones, completely…

To hear this poem touched Edmond deeply. Was he among the favourites of the gods? No, there was more suffering than pleasure in his life.

Mamadou had seen him and welcomed him at the door.
She wore a black dress which emphasised her voluptuous figure.

Her skin resembled dark cacao with milk.
"Bonsoir, my Queen of Sheba", he said, handing her
the *Macarons*. "You are sweeter than the Macarons."
She breathed a kiss on his cheek. "Old charmer," she said.

The bistro looked like an extension of the literary club on the first floor. The walls were covered with shelves filled with books donated by published writers, their anthologies, and books that had been through many hands and found a home here.

Some acquaintances were sitting at the bar. Gauthier with his flowing white hair under a wide-rimmed Calabrese hat.

Gauthier beckoned him over. He sat with a lady whom he introduced to Edmond as [a]erife. Black hair, tall, green eyes. Apparently, it's one of his new conquests.

Gauthier came straight to the point. "This is [a]erife from Turkey. She owns a café in the 10th arrondissement, I can recommend it. She wants to become a writer."

"Write," Edmond encouraged her, "writing is a therapy; write your heart out and empty your soul. What do you write? Prose, poetry?

"I want to write about my life."

"You'd better not. First, you are too young and have your life ahead of you, and second, most readers are only interested in other people's lives if they are glamorous or weird. You may draft your story in the third person as if you were gossiping about someone. People like gossip. Have you read *Orhan Pamuk*?"

"Yes, the Black Book. *Kara Kitap.*"

"I am a fan of *Pamuk*. This book is brilliant. It confronts the reader with puzzles, images, the melancholy of Istanbul, the weight of history, closed doors with secrets behind them, and the search for a missing person. *Pamuk* has a gift for bringing this to the surface. It reminds me of my happy times in Istanbul."

"Gauthier told me that you are a haiku poet."

"Yes, I can recommend it to non-native speakers; it is a Japanese discipline. Easy to learn, easy to write. You describe concise moments that shed light on details."

"It is strictly limited to 3 lines and follows a certain form, doesn't it?"

"Yes, three lines with 5, 7, 5 syllables, no title.
You see something and describe it in detail. A dewdrop on a blade of grass. A ray of sunlight on a leaf.

I give you an example. It also shows how to work around the number of syllables without being dogmatic:

bridge by night … three syllables
with the tram to Istanbul … we count seven syllables, perfect.
a full moon shines …four syllables, which is tolerable.

In Turkish: *gece köprüsü* …five syllables, it fits.
tramvay ile İstanbul'a …seven
dolunay parlar five syllables

"Beautiful. This interests me. How come you know Turkish?"

“Love,” I said.

”Aha,” was her reaction.

“By the way”, Edmond continued, “what about the rich and romantic Osmanian poetry.

Would it be worthwhile to follow this tradition and continue in a style adapted to our times?”

Serife nodded. “I remember the diwan poetry by *Hayatî Efendi*: *“Bir gül mü var bu gülşen i 'âlemde hârsız ' Is there a rose, in the rose garden of this world, without thorns?'* Thanks for the advice. Why invent the wheel again when we have such treasure?”

The owner of the bistro left the kitchen and approached the table. She was friendly and caring, like a mother. Even after midnight, she would serve omelettes, onion soup, or risotto. Her specialities were Sauerkraut and sausages (she was from Alsace).

We ordered risotto with porcini mushrooms.

Edmond resumed the conversation and told Gauthier, “I read the positive review of your recent poetry presentation in Lyon.”

Gauthier nodded: “I hope to have always been entertaining as a poet. Never forget that art and literature must primarily entertain. Only, you must never say this aloud.”

“Gauthier, what would you like to be if you were not a poet?”

“Dead,” he said.

Poet's Labour

Wordforge
looking for words
with a torch
in brain convolutions.

Penscreeches
on unfertilized paper
moves forward, pleaches
letters, text maker.

Sheetlimit
nightly thought
not to be timid
what dreams begot.

Brainanvil
no sound perceived,
my mind fights cavil -
a lot to be said.

Thoughtblaze
all imagination;
verse on a dais -
under scrutinization.

Self-doubt
Put the poem aside,
let it ferment for a while:
Good wine needs time.

Writing is Holy

When the Sufis dance,
their white whirling robes,
describe a circle,
the dervishes dance into a trance
to experience a deep mysticism,
the earthly
that encompasses all of us.

The Sufis revere poetry
and place it on a par
with religion, the deity,
see the soul as trans-local
and traceless
only to be seen
as a means of light,
guidance, invocation,
dedication and recitation,
its rhythm embraces
all humanity with love.

Hence they hold
the poets in high esteem,
the shavings of their sharpened pens
and their notepapers
are not thrown away,
but heat the water
with which the poet is washed
after his death.

The use of a pen or brush,
papyrus, parchment, or paper
stood at the beginning.
Printers, calligraphers,
preserve millennia-old techniques
and the scribes and poets
implemented
the gift of fire for hearth and forge,
to pass on a spiritual fire,
the flame of the word,
and with many different letters
to give the reader a means
to express and share
feelings and opinions.

All writing is sacred.
Every letter has a divine meaning.
We have written languages
for thousands of years:
Chinese characters,
Arabic, with its elegant sweep,
Latin in military order,
defining administration and state.

There is an old experience in all this.
In their free time, Chinese write
with water-soaked brushes
their characters, so artistic,
on the ground, let them evaporate
and rise as thin water vapour,
they disappear.

Poets move worlds, move thoughts,
move ideologies and religions.
The Sufis changed the
words of the Shahada,
la ilaha ill Allah (There is no deity but Allah)
to
la ilaha illa'l-'ishq (There is no deity but love).

This proves that poetry
is a mystical contemplation,
a concept of love,
interpretation of desires,
has a divine dimension,
circles around the eternal question:
Who am I?

Gone with Windblown Days

I love the contemporary prose
and poetry
presented by my Irish poet friends
and writing colleagues.
Some, however, might complain
about my awful accent as blow-in.
They applause politely and gently
not to cause any grief,
they are all nice
but think: what a cheek to
sail under the Irish flag,
this old ugly bag,
to inflict conglomerations on us
and we do not understand a bit.
Why is he not staying at home
to look at the falling calendar pages
and the last tumbling cherry blossoms,
the last for him,
he will never see them again,
next year,
because he might be dead.

Loss

Everything will pass.
We are marked by loss
by transience,
the loss of time
then follow in sequences
the various stages,
the loss of people, things,
the loss of grandparents, parents,
one's own age group, friends,
we lose eyesight, hearing, memory,
hair and beauty...

One becomes aware
that one is finite,
that one is passing away,
slowly disappear.

So, be attentive,
ignore the little pains,
one dies of many things,
not of lovesickness,
Life is full of sorrows
and worries.
That, too, will pass.
Only what you put on paper,
prose, poetry, literature,
will not be lost forever.

Poet's Dream

There is a reason, a trigger,
when I write a poem,
put it down on paper,
because on long nights
images form occasionally,
of lonely orchards
where seasonal fruits ripen
protected by fences and bushes.

Or a word and a thought
hold each other by the hand,
created in harmonious dreams,
nestling together, and it seems
they whisper of sunny places
near the blue sea.

Other times
it is as if rain gathered
in a leaf formation,
the burden puts it under tension;
like the strings of a sling
they catapult the water
into the air
like fears, nightmares,
accumulated
to come out of the darkness,
like a cry, a lament,
an accusation.

Often, however,
dark premonitions line up,
dance ring-a-ring-of roses
through the night
and fall, soot-blackened,
in letters onto the paper,
mixed with tears,
and create an image
like worlds of shadows,
like *Goya*'s paintings.

Translating the Irish Soul

I sit in front of my work,
contemplate over my draft,
a raft of haibun, an anthology,
describing the Irish scenery
in detail,
its flora and fauna, its beauty,
the Irish landscape as short prose,
in the tradition of *Matsuo Bashô*.

I want to give my German audience,
an idea of the wonderful sound,
to give them evidence
of a presumed-dead linguistic bijou,
the melody of the Irish *teanga*,
its cadence
to bring them closer to the Irish soul
with my stories and poems,
to let this mysticism resonate,
in their hearts,
describe a country
which I love and cherish.

At the text, I glance in awe:
Bothar Tuaithe, the Country Road....
and my eyes fill with tears:
My text in Irish,
like a consecration or incantation.
I learned about the family,
the people who created this,
their names like a rhyme:

Máirtin agus Mairin
Ailbne agus Róisin
Seán agus Tadgh

They live in the *Gaeltacht*:
The primordial ground,
refuge of this enchanting language,
the retreat
of a once-persecuted language,
wounded, suppressed, forbidden,
hidden.

We give it a new face, a meaning:
here, me, the poet,
there the guardians of the language.

Wishful Thinking of a German Poet

To be able to go somewhere,
to escape,
maybe to the seals, apes,
to Antarctica or the polar bears,
to a weather station
where you get a visit once a year
and the shotgun stands behind the door.
Or to Tierra de Fuegos.
To the Inuit?

Somewhere where you can write poetry
without words put on a gold scale.
Somewhere where you are spared
bureaucracy and administration
and the fucking state.
First, burn the tax returns,
provisions, regulations,
and leave the ashes behind.
Far away from civil servants
who sit behind their desks
and exercise power
and make a career at the expense of others.
Thinking up something every day
to make your life harder.

Rules and regulations are there
to keep people busy
so they cannot oppose,
have no time left,

to kill their creativity,
degrade them to ants
who only function and maintain the state.

Don’t accept this anymore,
resist,

become free again.

NON SCRIVERÒ PIÚ
I Will No Longer Write

Non scriverò piú
I will no longer write.
I can no longer fill the void
which yawns at me
like an abyss,
causing me an abysmal disgust,
and choking nausea
because of war, destruction
and hatred on streets, in towns
and media.

We have drifted apart,
lost ourselves in false romanticism,
only to realise
that almond trees no longer blossom
on scorched earth,
that a poisoned atmosphere
no longer permits a rosy dawn,
The gun thunder silenced the twittering birds.
Poets became narrow-minded extras.
It wounded the core of poetry
and creativity.

My pen has run out of ink,
just as a lack of moisture, lubrication,
makes joints ache

and nights sleepless,
in which images no longer emerge
that become verses at dawn.
The world is dead dark,
there is no more poetry.
Poets now walk without their masks.

We are at the end of *Dante's* Inferno.
Dante and *Virgil* saw beautiful things
that the sky bears.
'Io vidi de la cose belle che porta 'l ciel.'
We will no longer see them,
the chances are bleak.
After WW2 and Auschwitz,
the culture was deeply wounded,
disturbed and never recovered.
I hope we remember
and keep in mind.

Glossary

Hüzün sadness, sorrow, melancholy, a sad thought or feeling.

İstanbul'da bir güz. An autumn in Istanbul

Medress Madrasa is the Arabic word for any type of educational institution, secular or religious (of any religion), whether for elementary education or higher learning.

Obol The obol (Greek: *obolos*, Latin: *obolus*) was a form of ancient Greek currency and weight.
Charon's obol The deceased were buried with an obol placed in the mouth of the corpse, so that—once a deceased's shade reached Hades—they would be able to pay Charon for passage across the river Acheron or Styx.
Verdigris a bright bluish-green encrustation or patina formed on copper or brass by atmospheric oxidation, consisting of basic copper carbonate.
Ittar, also known as attar, is an essential oil derived from botanical or other natural sources.

Pegasus is a mythical winged stallion and one of the most recognised creatures in Greek mythology. Usually depicted as pure white in colour, Pegasus was a child of the Olympian god Poseidon.
Pegasus became associated with poetry around the 19th century as the originator or fountainhead of sources from which the poets gained inspiration.

Matsuo Bashō was the most famous Japanese poet of the Edo period. During his lifetime, Bashô was recognized for his works in the collaborative haikai no renga form; today, after centuries of commentary, he is recognized as the greatest master of haiku.

Teanga, Irish language

Bothar Tuaithe, the Country Road

Máirtin ***agus*** *Mairin*
Ailbne agus Róisin
Seán agus Tadgh

Irish first names connected with agus = and

Gaeltacht Irish speaking region

Published:

Home Green Home, published by Southern Arizona Press USA and

Time for Verses by Cyberwit.net - India's Largest Publishing House.

He writes also under his Irish pen name: Eadbhard McGowan

Do not hesitate to contact me:

Eadbhardmcgowan@gmx.com

www.ingramcontent.com/pod-product-compliance
Ingram Content Group UK Ltd.
Pitfield, Milton Keynes, MK11 3LW, UK
UKHW041314190726
13845UKWH00025B/257

9 788119 654055